SOCIAL MEDIA FOR PARENTS

Table of Contents

Introduction

Globally, we spend around 9.5 billion hours on social media each year. As more people are connected and corporations develop more immersive platforms, this number increases exponentially. It is no surprise that social media influences our society in diverse ways. Depending on how the media is used, this could be positive... or negative.

It is important to note the intent of the various apps, and the focus for which they were developed, as we try to understand the extent to which they may influence our children.

There are many capabilities to these platforms, and learning how to identify them can help in understanding how various developments may influence thinking and behavior.

As a not so techy parent to teenagers, I have attempted to keep up with the various social media that are being used today. If you are as confused as I was when I started this project, keep reading. You'll have a better understanding of the most popular social media platforms today, as well as the features of each.

1. The Business

The social media world starts long before opening any apps. Although the original driving force for the creation of these apps would likely originate from a genuine desire to innovate and provide the world with something helpful, somewhere along the line, it all just became… business.

At the start of their lifetimes, we can presume that most of these companies have the genuine intention of bridging the gap between how people communicate with one another. However, as time progresses, their goals start to shift and things can become controversial, even for the companies themselves.

The point at which most of these companies transition from innovation to business can be seen as the point at which they monetize. With investors and shareholders seeking a profit on their money, there comes a time in a tech company's lifespan when it needs to turn a profit. This often leads to a perceivable shift in future updates, changing the company's decision-making from an experience-orientated mentality to a revenue orientated one.

Ads

The primary way social media companies like Meta (Formerly Facebook) and Twitter make money is through selling advertising. They say, "If you're not paying for the product, the product is you." Kind of a chilling thought, isn't it? That these social media companies profit off our attention is why their applications are focused on satisfying advertiser demands above user demands.

Over 60% of social media users find ads to be distracting, intrusive, and excessive.

Ads show up frequently, and it can be quite frustrating. Forbes says "the average person sees <u>10,000 ads</u> every single day." How is that even possible?!

Also, the tricky way that advertisements are embedded to look like regular content makes identifying ads on each application somehow different. Spending some time on each social media platform and keeping an eye out for when a post is subtly marked with the words "sponsored" or "promoted" can help in learning how to identify advertising.

Within a little time, you will become familiar with how the ads are presented and the different methods marketers use. For our purposes here, it's important to know what type of ads are being shown to our children.

Algorithms

We won't get into the details of how algorithms work as that could be a lengthy and very technical discussion. Let's just cover the basics.

Social media giants don't want us skipping or scrolling past ads, though. So, they develop algorithms.

Each application has an algorithm, and generally, these algorithms learn about what each user likes to watch, buy, and engage with on the internet. This is done to show you more of what you like and to tailor advertisements that would apply to you.

Unfortunately, these algorithms are not perfect. Many of these apps prioritize the already successful content by pushing them to the top of your feed (even if it's content you didn't subscribe to seeing) to maximize advertising and thus revenue on said content. You can see how this might trouble parents – what exactly are our kids being sold?

When you use social media, experiment with the algorithm and how it tailors itself to you. It's quite interesting to watch. Start engaging (liking, sharing, or commenting) on a very specific type of content that interests you for a few days (e.g. marine life) and observe how the algorithm will start showing you more and more marine-based content. Then watch a different type of content (e.g. cars) and watch how the algorithm will show you both marine and car-related content. The more content of a specific variety you view, the more the algorithm will show it to you.

Devices

With social media being so easily accessible through our phones, laptops, and tablets, a culture of "instant gratification" has developed amongst those who spend a lot of time on these apps – especially our kids who spent this time on social media during developmental stages of their life.

If you are unfamiliar with what "instant gratification" is, it is "the tendency to forego future benefits to get a less rewarding but more immediate benefit." Essentially, social media is an easy way to get dopamine (a chemical that's released in your brain that makes you feel good) without having to put in very much effort. If young people become more acclimated to getting whatever they want, as soon as they want it... this is a recipe for disaster as it relates to our future generations!

The average user has about 6-7 hours of screen time per day. This is quite substantial when you consider the average person spends only 16 hours of their day awake! So basically, our kiddos spend half of their waking day on social media getting quick and easy access to dopamine.

It may be beneficial to look into methods of teaching children the benefit of delayed gratification in that they may have to work a certain amount of time before receiving rewards as then it may be a longer-lasting or more satisfying. (But that is a topic for another book).

For now, let's dive deeper into some of the most popular social media applications and the various positive and negative aspects we may encounter as our children use these apps.

2. Facebook

With Facebook, the original goal was to "give people the power to build community and bring the world closer together." Facebook currently has nearly 3 billion users, so it is safe to assume that they (more or less) succeeded on this front.

Founded by Mark Zuckerberg, Facebook is easily the most successful social media and was the initial ripple that drove the world of social media today. It was innovative, and it filled a gap in a unique market where there was a lot of room for growth.

The application can be used on phones, computers, and tablets. It is relatively similar across devices, with a few changes in placing various windows and buttons.

Facebook is now known as "Meta." They have adjusted their focus to "bringing the metaverse to life and helping people connect, find communities and grow businesses." (If you aren't aware of what the metaverse is, it is "a virtual-reality space in which users can interact with a computer-generated environment and other users"). They are trying to significantly enhance the level of emersion that we experience with the application.

If this environment becomes as immersive as they hope, they will gain significantly more access to personal information, and with advertising being their primary source of income, their platform can be revolutionary but poses dangers we must be aware of.

Groups

As a Facebook user, the **Groups** on Facebook are one of the most useful features of the platform. It is very useful because users with similar interests can commune and share ideas, experiences, or whatever they like. As you can presume, I am a part of various writing groups that allow me to share and promote my work, get feedback, and network with others.

One of the key ways to do this on Facebook is in "Groups." Groups allow users to build communities around specific ideas and beliefs. Etc. and do exactly what they had intended, "build a community".

In fact, groups can be made private to control who is allowed in the group and varying levels degrees of engagement (e.g. only certain users may post in groups. Others can only like and comment). Allowing users to be selective of who joins based on age, beliefs, and friendship circles. Etc. for safety or privatization.

It would be important to keep notice of which groups your children are a part of, as some can be dedicated to sharing misinformation, getting private information from other users, sharing harmful content or ideas, and it is often used to co-ordinate events (of which many can be protests or rallies).

As you can see, there are give-and-takes to the aspects of Facebook groups. Its attributes can be used for both positive and negative influence, so be mindful of the groups that you and your children are participating in. The community has a powerful ability to influence one's thinking.

The below information explains the basic "parts" of Facebook.

Messaging

Facebook users can directly message other users either one-on-one or in a group. This is often referred to as a **Direct Message** (aka a "DM").

This allows users an additional level of privacy in their communication, as this is a purely private conversation between those involved. Although these conversations are not publicized (unless users post images of the conversation) it is often a portal for cyberbullying. So it would be important to monitor who is directly messaging you and your children, as it may be valuable to delete or report various types of messages.

It is also important to watch out for bots through Facebook's messenger system as many users use bots to notify their communities and audiences of various information. However, bots are often used for spamming users with useless information or with links to get their information. When bots send links, it is important to be certain of the link you are visiting, as many bots will link you to a website to steal your information through your Facebook account, which has resulted in cases of identity theft.

Live Streaming

Facebook allows users to stream live videos to the platform, allowing for various gamers, podcasts, and events to be viewed within the application. Users can live stream with another party, allowing for multiple individuals to participate.

I would encourage you to look at some live streams yourself to see what's popular on the platform. If your child is streaming live, it could be valuable to understand what type of content they are streaming and who is engaging with their streams, as they can still be a source of cyberbullying. Live streams are also usually public, allowing anyone in the world to view in. Scary, right?

In the past, Facebook has had issues with censorship on its platform concerning live streaming. For example, there have been instances in the past where individuals in the U.S have streamed footage of deadly shootings directly to Facebook. This can be a source of trauma and distress for anyone watching and I would highly recommend being mindful of content like this, as it is quite tough to regulate as they are being streamed live and Facebook can only stop the stream once moderators have flagged the video as inappropriate or the viewers report it (which usually takes some time).

Besides that, many people have developed careers, promoted their work, or just engaged with friends and family through live streaming on Facebook.

Stories

Stories are a feature added to Facebook that was inspired by Snapchat. Users can post 15-second stories, which can be videos or photos. These posts disappear after 24 hours and will no longer be viewable by other users. Stories can often be found by viewing a user's profile and clicking on their profile picture if there is a colorful border around the image.

Stories (because of their disappearing nature) can often be used to quickly and discreetly post misinformation or harmful imagery. It is also common for images or videos to go viral on stories by users copying a story they saw and sharing it on their own stories if they resonate with it, somehow.

Coupled with the fact that it is significantly easier and faster to post to stories, it is a feature with a lot of activity that can easily go unnoticed.

The type of stories you or your children see will primarily be determined by who you are following or who your "friends" are on the platform.

Video Content

Facebook has made an enormous commitment to prioritize video content across its platform. Video content engages users for a longer time, and videos encourage users to continue scrolling if they are satisfied with the content they are seeing. This is important to know because social media platforms focusing on video content generally result in users being more inclined to post videos of their faces and users spending significantly more time on them.

Facebook as an application is constantly changing, as these changes often affect how the various communities engage with one another. Video content holds the general threats that we identified as cyberbullying, invasion of privacy, or identity theft, but most of the controversy that will arise will be because of the app's culture.

Culture

The culture of the application is the most important aspect to observe and note. Due to the groups that exist within Facebook, there is perceivable segregation and isolation of beliefs and opinions. This often leads to Facebook users being seen as very argumentative when they are challenged on these beliefs or opinions.

Discussion and debate can be powerful. However, this is not what you will predominantly come across on the app. The discussion topics are often surrounding very controversial subjects, notably politics.

Facebook users spending time in circles that affirm pre-existing beliefs results in often hostile and intense interactions when users react to public information released on varying news outlets, ads, or even public posts. Reacting and commenting on news and misinformation is very common on Facebook.

This comes back to advertising because it is not only companies promoting products or services on these platforms. It would be good to monitor whether these advertisements are appearing on your children's social media.

Controversies

I would suggest monitoring some controversies that surround Facebook, as this will give you an idea of where the platform is headed, as well as how it affects the users.

I briefly touched on how Facebook uses your information to influence advertising. This information is often sold to politicians and is used to influence you when making important decisions. Many countries have become savvier of this and have incorporated laws to minimize how much control Facebook and other companies can have over your data, as well as what they can and cannot do with it.

Countries like South Africa and the United Kingdom have implemented very strict laws that provide the public control over their information. Allowing users to request for their information to be removed at their own will, and if they are unaware of the data these companies hold, the companies are required to destroy the data after a certain period (the details of these laws vary, depending on which country you are located; it's a must research the privacy laws in your country).

In the United States, laws have been implemented to protect children from advertising. This is still far off from what is necessary to protect users' information and the various ways it is used to sway public opinion.

Another controversy that surrounds Facebook is its apparent monopolization of the market. Recently, Facebook has attempted to purchase a variety of competitors in emerging markets for either for research or simply eliminating competition. A few of these purchases have been rejected by the Federal Trade Commission. Facebook has acquired a variety of companies, such as Instagram, WhatsApp, and Oculus (A Virtual Reality gaming company). They have also been known for attempting to purchase Snapchat in the past. However, Snapchat owners refused to sell. Facebook then decided to essentially copy the Snapchat concept by incorporating "Stories" across Facebook, Instagram, and WhatsApp. Some see this as a shady move, as it seemed Facebook was willing to do whatever was necessary to get rid of the competition.

As the largest social media platform, Facebook has a lot of influence on our society today, and it can be very beneficial to spend some time in this world to gain an understanding of the culture and how it may be affecting your children.

3. Instagram

Instagram is one of the most popular social media sites in the world. It was created with the intention of "providing people and artists with a free photo and video sharing app that allows a visual storyteller to share their creative ideas." Instagram is the most successful image-sharing social media platform because of a variety of features and the overall layout of the application.

Initially, Instagram would show the content that you post to the audience that follows you. The more followers you have, the more engagement you would get on each of your posts. Eventually, they adjusted how this process works and started focusing on promoting what was most popular. This led to a massive decline in engagement amongst users who weren't able to compete with more popular influencers and celebrities. Users were no longer simply being shown the content of creators they followed, but were merely being shown posts that already had a lot of engagement to them. As a user trying to follow a specific creator, it can be frustrating to see you've missed a month of their posts for no apparent reason.

The point at which this change took place can be identified not too long after 2012 when Instagram was bought by the parent company "Facebook" (now known as 'Meta'). The reason Instagram was purchased by Facebook is that Instagram was a legitimate threat to the success of Facebook. Instagram was motivated to sell because Facebook was threatening to mimic Instagram's formula and create its version of the app on Facebook.

Facebook wanted to monetize Instagram, so back to advertising. Similar to Facebook, this has become Instagram's primary source of income as well. They place targeted advertisements between the posts on your feed, making ads a quarter of the content seen on Instagram by users.

Features

Instagram is not as complex as Facebook, nor does it hold as many features as its parent application. There are a few key tabs on the app on which people spend the most time. These would be the home feed, stories and the explore tab (other features include Direct Messaging and the Instagram marketplace).

Instagram Feed

The main Instagram feed is the first page you will see when you open the application. Here, you will see a variety of content. Starting with the most liked content from the creators that you follow. Once creators get a certain amount of engagement, Instagram will start showing it to more people.

You will also come across "Sponsored" content on your feed. These are ads placed by companies that are trying to promote their service or product as well as users who are trying to promote their content to a larger audience and gain more traction. Many users turn their content into ads because it has become significantly more difficult to grow an audience over the years.

Last, Instagram has begun "suggested" content in which content from certain creators is placed on your feed, regardless of whether you follow them, because the algorithm has determined it to be content you will most likely engage with. Depending on whether or not you engage with the content will determine if you'll see more of it or not.

Stories

Stories on Instagram are essentially the same as the Stories on Facebook. The difference is the sub-features available in the stories on Instagram that allow for significantly more creativity in a user's posts and features to allow certain users to funnel viewers to websites or other apps.

This feature is far more popular on Instagram than it is on Facebook and was incorporated when Facebook wanted to take on Snapchat. The stories on Instagram also have more of a tendency to achieve varying levels of "virality" and also are more shareable.

There are trends on Instagram in which some images or videos are shared straight from the feed to stories, boosting the engagement on the original post and adding a layer of visibility to the content. This allows for images and videos that are posted on Instagram to go viral while still maintaining a link to a source.

However, because of the simplicity of these levels of virality, it also becomes significantly easier to bully people and share content that harms mental health. When this negative content is shared, it becomes easy to affect many users in a variety of ways.

Explore

The explore tab on Instagram is the most effective way to view new content that you have not engaged with yet, and it provides the opportunity to see how your algorithm has been tailored (based on the content that is being shown to you).

Content that is on the explore page isn't just tailored to you, but it is also the most successful content of the genres that you are most interested in.

The primary purpose of this feature is to allow you to find new content based on the parameters that you would prefer, such as location, subject, videos or images and to find people you know by typing their usernames.

Marketplace

Instagram is massively popular for the lifestyle content on the application and this has led to the decision to incorporate a marketplace into the app. The marketplace is generally used by brands and high-end influencers to promote clothing, jewelry, and other products that can be purchased through the app.

Many teens may feel obligated to make purchases based on the most popular content they are seeing. This often leads to social pressure to follow in these trends.

Audience

The large majority of Instagram users are between the ages of 18 and 29, and 68% are female. This is important because of the psychological effects that these applications have on mental health and perceptions of themselves.

Many users garner high engagement because they have enough money to travel or purchase products that draw attention to the app because of their association with success and wealth. The application has a culture of high engagement for individuals who can be seen as physically attractive. Often, users feel pressured to have a certain appearance or to purchase certain products because they feel as though it's necessary to draw attention to social media and not come across as "weird" for not participating.

Social media has a huge effect on mental health, but Instagram has a unique impact because of the importance of pictures and the publication of engagement. If one posts on Instagram and doesn't get much engagement, this can feel embarrassing and demotivating, encouraging users to adjust their appearance and daily life to attain more engagement.

It is difficult to avoid comparing themselves to other users. This can cause many issues for people because they are unaware of a creator's life beyond the post they've just engaged with. But these posts can be highly suggestive of success, wealth, beauty, and happiness that viewers start to ask themselves questions such as "Why aren't I that successful?" or "How can I be that happy?" and this is very dangerous for mental wellbeing.

A good point for us parents to make – what you see on Instagram (or TV) isn't "real" life and isn't always true.

Culture

Because lifestyle content is the most successful on the application, there is an issue of perception on Instagram that occurs naturally among every user posting on the app, which is more harmful than it seems. It is the basic idea of taking multiple selfies to then use the "best one" and the "best one" can simply be described as the image that maintains the most beauty standards, thus making the image more likable.

The application subconsciously drives users to identify and mimic the most successful content on the app. If you take a moment on the app and observe the content that appears on your feed, you will most likely begin seeing consistencies amongst the posts and what drives certain levels of success to them.

4. Snapchat

Founded in 2011, Snapchat is one of the most popular social media platforms among teens. All the "Story" functionalities that you see on Instagram, Facebook, WhatsApp, and TikTok are based on the original features of Snapchat.

Snapchat was made to be a "private, person-to-person photo sharing application" which can now be used to send videos, have live video calls, direct messaging, share stories, and include a wide variety of augmented reality filters. Today, Snapchat is at the forefront of these augmented reality filters that are very popular on different social media such as TikTok and Instagram, despite the efforts from competitors to mimic this outcome.

There are about 330 million daily active users on the application every day. And it is steadily growing, increasing from 309 million in the third quarter of 2021. Most Snapchat users are between the ages of 18-25 and therefore there is such a concentration on entertainment news and celebrity culture. Although on a personal note, Snapchat seems to be the ONLY app used by my teenage daughter and friends.

Features

Snapchat boasts a lot of features that allow its users to interact with one another in a variety of intimate ways. It is very common for engagement between two users to last a long time and occur in a variety of ways as Snapchat encourages users to maintain "streaks" in which they consistently engage with each other for exchange of various badges that are displayed on a user's profile.

With Snapchat, I would highly recommend monitoring the people your child may be engaging with on the app. Many of these engagements take the form of temporary images sent between users, and this means users rarely maintain a record of their messages.

Snap Camera

The Snap camera can take images and videos that can be sent directly to users or broadcast to friends as stories. This is the primary way in which users send messages to one another as they can type or draw text and images into the photo they have taken with the snap camera. Users can also add filters to images that allow them to overlay colors or various other interactive features to make them more interesting or relevant to the conversation. These filters are called "lenses" on Snapchat.

It is important to note that even though these images may disappear after a selected time, receivers may still screenshot these images to save them for any reason and Snapchat can only notify the sender that the image has been screenshot.

This may become a concern if users are sending each other provocative or inappropriate messages as a sender may have intended for it to be private and disappear, but ultimately, they do not have control of this, making the appeal of disappearing images less impactful.

Snap Map

The Snap map is a feature that allows users to share their live location with other users that they add as friends. This feature is only active while Snapchat is open and can be changed into "ghost mode" in which a user chooses not to share their location.

This can be dangerous for obvious reasons as people may not intend to be sharing their location with their friend's list, but it can be viewed by anyone using the app at the same time. It would be important to look at whether or not your child is doing this as the possibility is high and it may not be the safest feature in protecting privacy.

Memories Screen

Snapchat has a feature that allows a user to save any of the images that they have sent and view them later.

Apps like Instagram and Facebook have copied this feature, making it more common to remind users of previous experiences and re-share them.

Chat Screen

Even though images are the fundamental mode of communication on Snapchat, users still have the option to communicate in a group chat or one-on-one in text-style chatting. This feature saves images and further allows users to engage with one another by allowing them to directly react or respond to images with a message.

These messages are deleted once users leave the conversation; however, users may still screenshot these texts as an alternative way of saving them. Through this screen, users can also live chat with one another like on FaceTime.

This is where the depth of conversation can take place between users and knowing who your children are communicating with the most may be useful to track by observing their SnapStreaks. This can be done without invading the privacy of their conversations, but by asking who the users are that they are engaging.

SnapStreak

A SnapStreak is determined by users sending each other images daily and can be influenced by additional factors such as how many images are shared. It is usually represented by an emoji next to the friend's username.

Snapchat also places the chat list in chronological order of engagement, so the user placed at the top is often the user being messaged the most.

It can be very addictive to maintain these streaks with users, as many levels can be achieved, and it is quite fun to keep them. This keeps users on the app and forms encourages deep relationships, which can be good and bad depending on who is communicating.

Discover

Similar to other apps, the "discover' "tab allows users to engage with the most popular images being shared on the app and view a variety of

Snapchat-specific content created by independent and corporate curators.

You can also view users' stories, which can be viewed by all friends but expire after 24 hours. Stories can also be viewed publicly depending on their success and will be displayed on the spotlight tab.

Culture

Snapchat focuses heavily on celebrity news and virality. Snapchat also encourages a mentality of impermanence, as most of the modes of communication expire and delete after varying periods, and this may encourage users to behave more recklessly in the images and messages that they send.

In fact, various content creators make a sub-culture of nudity and pornographic content available on the platform and it becomes very easy for underage users to view this content by simply following people that are sharing it. This coincides with the focus on celebrity culture and gossip to keep users engaged. Explicit content, like Instagram, is beneficial to the platform's engagement because people of various ages and genders engage with what they find physically appealing.

Controversies

It is very easy to have intimate conversations with a stranger on Snapchat, and like any app, it comes with its dangers. Personal information can be easily accessed on Snapchat unless personal settings are changed. Images and conversations are not completely private or safe from being saved, and it is easy to access pornographic content on the app with a little system for controlling this. Many people have been scammed through this app and others by sending erotic images to other users who then threaten to sell these images for money. Users of all apps affect mental health; however, Snapchat may cause various issues because of its heavy focus on celebrity entertainment and viral content.

It would be valuable to discuss the danger of engaging with strangers online with your children while also getting to know who they are chatting with. The culture of the app is also very focused on entertainment news and informing your child of the effects this may have on how they think and socialize can raise their awareness of the factors and they can learn to avoid them.

5. Tik Tok

TikTok was previously known as an app called "Musical.ly" that focused on music videos in which users could lip sync or react to their favorite songs. In 2017, a company called "Bytedance" (A Chinese internet technologies company) purchased "musical.ly" and renamed it "TikTok."

The app is now the fastest growing app, with over 1 billion users worldwide. It allows users to post short video content (as long as it abides by the rules). Most of the content is under 3 minutes long, which allows users to endlessly scroll through a massive database of content.

A lot of the content is focused on being entertaining, however, because it no longer requires users to post a video with music, there is also a lot of content that has no particular focus. Comedy skits, reacting videos (in which users record themselves watching and reacting to other content), educational videos (in which users may specialize in different topics to educate anyone interested), "Meltdown" videos (Which is a common trend in which a user shares a video of themselves going through a hard time), inspirational videos (in which different moguls and gurus may inspire their audiences to achieve success) and many more.

TikTok was created to be a social media platform for "creating, sharing and discovering short videos." A lot of users on the app use it merely to be entertained. However, TikTok users desire "virality" more than users on other platforms. This is because the app prioritizes being engaging and keeping users on the app above monetization as it is primarily funded and fuelled by the Chinese government. This results in TikTok being a source of much controversy as many are unsure of what the Chinese government uses the app for.

The musical aspect of TikTok also makes it extremely popular (even though it is not specialized in musical content). It is quite common for pop songs or previously unknown songs to go viral globally through the application as there are many trends on the app that revolve around a particular song (generally a short portion of the song) that users will engage with, similarly (essentially the song is associated with a meme).

TikTok being the most popular app also means that it has the most satisfied user base, and this is especially because of its algorithm. They also have a huge foothold on the video content that is found on other apps as videos are often saved from TikTok and then posted on other applications (keep an eye out for the TikTok logo on some videos, the logo being watermarked on a video means it was saved from the platform).

Most users on TikTok are between the ages of 18 – 24, but it also engages youth from 13 to 17 as well. This means that TikTok has a massive effect on the development of the youth and how they think. It would be very important to understand what content your kids are engaging with, as it may drastically affect their mentality and their mental health.

Video sharing

Sharing videos on TikTok is quite simplistic as the app specializes in video content. Aside from uploading videos, users can react to other videos by recording themselves and watching the video they would like to react to. They can "duo" other videos, which are common with music trends in which a user plays a guitar melody, and another user adds to it by videoing themselves singing. Users can add to the end of other users' videos. This is known as a "stitch" and they are consistently adding new ways for users to expand on one another's content.

These aspects make it highly engaging as videos can cross between users; making it very simple to create content and piggyback on viral videos. With TikTok, users can edit quite advanced videos, depending on the extent of their creativity, and several filters can help users create unique content and potentially new trends. These filters are like Snapchat, however, there is a lot more use for these filters depending on the trends that they may be associated with. On TikTok's editor, users can also cut multiple clips together, add voiceovers or text, and overlay music.

Users can also record multiple clips in the app through the camera tab and live stream to the app.

Music and Dancing

The musical aspect of TikTok is very important in viral videos and trends. This makes the music industry extremely interested in creating music and video content that attracts attention to these applications. Some would say that TikTok is more likely to adjust the application based on what record labels desire above advertisers on the platform.

Many people have had their music careers elevated on TikTok because of one of their songs going viral. Once it does, there is often a dance that may be associated with the song. Most of these dances are simplistic and achievable by anybody, but occasionally some of the trends may lean towards a mature audience.

Stories

Similar to other apps, TikTok has also adopted "stories" feature in which users can post disappearing videos or photos of themselves to their followers or whoever may appear on their profile. TikTok has done nothing different with its stories feature as it is merely a strategy of satisfying users by providing them with more to engage with.

Additional Features

Users can also "direct message" one another and exchange content or simply have text-based conversations. Users can search for specific content, trends, or users using the search bar and they can organize content according to what is posted by friends, what is trending, or who they are following.

TikTok may add more features over time, however, they are heavily focused on the core of what their application is (Video content) and if they do not fall into the trap that other platforms have in diverging from this focus, TikTok is likely to become the largest social media application.

Controversies

Even though TikTok has very few features, it is one of the most influential apps. This also makes it one of the most dangerous, as there are many aspects to the video content that can harm users.

The biggest lingering controversy is around the ownership of the application. It is ultimately owned by the Chinese government, and it has resulted in confusing political intentions through their use of the app. Many believe that China is using the application to gain data and monitor the behavior and interest of all of its users. What they may do with this information is unknown, but many people perceive the app as a method of social destabilization. Without getting too political, it may be possible that TikTok is used to draw the attention of the youth and encourage them to prioritize virality and popularity above more standard expectations. There are a lot of youngsters who see education or getting a job as less important if they achieve a monetizable follower count. It is important to note that this information is unknown. It could just as easily be western propaganda against TikTok as it is influential and enjoyed by a billion people.

If you use TikTok, I encourage you to look up the type of content that achieves virality in China. It is often content with good behavior and hard work that Chinese users are supposedly engaged with. This could be because of China attempting to influence how the youth think, or it could just result from the national culture. Similar to how celebrity and stardom may be a huge part of American culture. TikTok has focused meticulously on ensuring people see content based on their location. This initially started as a national and transnational approach to displaying content and has become more specifically on local, smaller regions. This hints at their control of the spread of information/content as this does not sound harmful but may expose people to personal information (such as general location). If I post on TikTok, I would rather prefer people weren't able to figure out which city I'm in, let alone which neighborhood!

Another issue that TikTok faces is pedophilia. This occurs because of the large demographic of minors using the platform and posting videos of themselves dancing or even posting videos speaking to their followers. It can often turn out that those followers are much older than expected. They will often leave comments on videos with requests for certain types of content to be posted. TikTok has a feature that allows users to directly respond to comments with a video and users asking a TikToker to upload a video doing a trending dance happens regularly and can appear innocent. I would highly advise keeping an eye on the content your child is posting to the platform, as well as the comments that are left and responded to on their videos. This can be achieved by creating an account of your own to view your child's content without having to ask them every time. It could also be valuable to make them aware of these dangers and inform them you will be monitoring their content without being overbearing. Accounts can be banned through the comments section from viewing further content from a TikToker through the TikToker's account.

Hate speech is also a dangerous aspect of TikTok. A lot of bullying can take place in the comments section of a TikToker's posts if they say something that is not socially acceptable. Various influencers misinform their viewers and monetize harmful behaviors by targeting the insecurities of younger viewers. If a TikToker amasses a following by saying something hateful, the audience responds to criticisms of the TikToker by bullying. This shows the influence certain TikTokers have and the mentality of children and teenagers can be negatively affected by this.

Lastly, TikTok can also expose younger users to mature content. It is a typical place for various nude models to "promote their work" to potential audiences and although TikTok is constantly removing these pages, it is quite easy to just create a new TikTok account and keep posting. There is an age restriction setting on the app and on your child's phone that can avoid that kind of content appearing on their feed. I would advise you to look into these settings and activate them.

6. Reddit

Reddit has defined its purpose as a "social media news website and forum where content is curated and promoted by site members through voting." These "forums" are the equivalent of public groups that anyone can join (unless made private). The forums are topical, and users can upload and comment on posts of a similar variety.

The company was founded in 2005. Despite this, the application has changed a little beyond its policy; it even offers users the opportunity to use the original design of the website. It currently has around 430 million users worldwide who are known as "Redditors" of whom the majority are between the ages of 18 and 29.

Reddit differs from other social media sites and comes with various "freedoms" that make the platform somewhat unbiased. Essentially, if users aren't posting anything illegal on these forums (aka. Sub-reddits), then it is fair game. This means that you can find almost anything on the app, depending on what you're brave enough to search for.

Home Page

The home page shows the most popular posts on the different subreddits that users follow. On this feed, they can also see the most popular posts across all subreddits and see recommendations of other subreddits you may enjoy.

Sub-Reddits

Sub-reddits are the forums or groups that users create to share the content of a specific category with one another. A subreddit like r/funny will comprise posts by users that they think are funny and opt to share in the forum. Other users can then react and "upvote" or "downvote" posts that they like or don't like. The posts with the most upvotes will be shown to the most people and appear on a user's home page.

There are millions of subreddits with a variety of categories as their focus. This expands on what was previously mentioned about Reddit being a platform that allows almost any type of content unless it is illegal. Sub-reddits range from pages such as r/aww (which will show users cute animal posts) to a page such as r/peoplefuckingdying (which will share posts of people losing their lives). Pornography is also easy to come across on Reddit with a variety of subreddits focusing on certain types of pornography.

If your child is using Reddit, it would be very important to activate the age restriction setting that can be found in the app and monitor the subreddits that your child may be following. It is very easy for someone to come across some of these harmful posts if they do well in their subreddits and appear on the front page (posts from r/peoplefuckingdying can often appear on a user's home page because of their popularity) although they do a good job of ensuring that pornographic content doesn't appear in the same vein.

Karma

Reddit has a few features that differentiate it from other social media forms (such as its subreddit structure). They also have a method in which they score different users with a system called "Karma." This encourages users to stick to the rules and engage with the platform. Various subreddits have their own set of rules about what users can post into the forums and say in the comments. Users will lose karma if they do something that breaks the rules, and they will gain Karma for posting or commenting and getting upvotes on either. The more upvotes you get, the more Karma you get.

This can make the app somewhat addictive as it provides more rewards for getting engagement from others. Upvotes can be seen as "likes," whilst karma is an additional way of rewarding users.

Moderators

All moderators are users who have the role of moderators, or they are bots that are prompted to remove content or comments based on the rules of the subreddit. Moderators may sound like a good idea, but it turns out it may not have been the best option for a website like Reddit. They have essentially given certain users the right to police what other users say throughout the platform. Some human moderators oversee hundreds of subreddits, making it very easy for them to enforce their own opinions onto the platform. It is quite common for comments and controversial statements to be removed by moderators, which can be a good thing as it can protect users from harmful behavior and bullying, but it diverges the platform further away from being a source of free speech.

Redditors are motivated to remove posts and comments that they are not interested in, as they are often paid to advertise on their subreddits by advertisers. This often results in comments and posts being deleted in the event users within a subreddit are unhappy with what is being marketed to them. Often, moderators remove these comments that are in protest as they have all the power to do so, and it looks better to advertisers when all the comments are positive. So, there are positive and negative aspects that can come from moderators, but in the community of Reddit, it is predominantly seen as a restriction method.

Messaging

Like other social platforms, users can send one another direct messages. This means that users can respond to posts or comments by sending a message. On Reddit, direct messaging is often a source of bullying or even scamming. Most users try to comment on posts to gain karma, and this often requires them to water down their opinions or responses to what others say so they are not removed from comment sections. Usually, the best way to voice your unfiltered opinion on the platform is through direct messaging someone who you disagree with and engaging in a "conversation" on a more personal level.

Additionally, Sub-reddits also use direct messaging to notify users of various information, such as when their comment or post gets removed.

Culture

As I noted before, the culture of Reddit aimed to focus on freedom of speech. This community likes to engage in discussion, say and post whatever they want while expecting those who are "offended" or "disagree" to simply move along and find content they would rather engage with.

It's aim to be an open stream of conversation and interests. However, many people who like to engage with Reddit as it is currently structured understand the value of bullying and harassing users who say something outside of mainstream opinions. These users are often very argumentative and try to enforce their opinions because they understand the app would align with their views and potentially ban users who disagree.

Controversies

Reddit controversies are centered on making decisions that the community is unhappy with. When the company had sold to "Wired," the restriction of speech on the platform began, and this is because of investor interests. As time went on, users were more and more concerned about these corporate decisions restricting everyone's freedoms. From here, the investors wanted to advertise on the platform as a mode of monetization and this is where moderators were introduced to ensure a level of control on what is being said so that advertisers are happy. This grew and grew until it reached a point in which Reddit then took a large investment from Tencent (One of the biggest companies in China is owned by the Chinese government). This was terribly negative by the community, as they believe there would come a lot of restrictions on what can be said and shared about China. Eventually, this came to be the case as users would share damning information against the Chinese government to inform the community and these posts would be removed. Even if it was a post highlighting something inhumane, that was committed by China. The freedom of speech mentality has fallen so far from Reddit that it has turned into a platform no different from the others. The major downfall came from investment and monetization, as this is always the source of where free speech has to be restricted for advertisers to be satisfied. Noting a shift from prioritizing the community to prioritizing the income.

7. YouTube

YouTube was founded in 2005 to provide a "video sharing service where users can watch, like, share, comment and upload their videos". Google purchased it in 2006, and YouTube quickly became the second biggest search engine in the world.

Unlike TikTok or Instagram, YouTube is a combination of a social media platform and a search engine.

One of the most successful forms of content on the platform right now is kid's content. Many children become obsessed with different animated shows, unboxing videos of toys, and even child dance crews. YouTube probably has the largest range of users, with its core audience being between the ages of 15 and 35 years old and a total user base of 2 billion.

It is safe to say that YouTube is not the place it used to be, and even though it is going through many changes within its community that different YouTubers (users who make a career of posting on YouTube) are unhappy with and trying to change. This is largely due to YouTube being owned by the massive holding company, Alphabet. YouTube used to be a website that acted as an introduction to the dark web. There never used to be any manageable systems in place to prevent racism, homophobia, hate speech, and pornography, and something that was disturbingly common on the app was terrorists filming themselves killing journalists or hostages and posting it right to YouTube.

The platform has changed a lot and now that it is one of the biggest search engines in the world, Google went through a lot of effort to ensure it is maintainable so that investors and advertisers are happy. It faces similar issues to other platforms, but YouTube relies significantly more on the success of content that its user's post. Since ads are placed on videos, if these content creators are unhappy with the platform, then they will often find other means of monetization. YouTubers have signed sponsorship deals outside of YouTube and placing the ads in the video themselves. This allows them to skip YouTube as the middleman (who would take most of the money from advertising) and maximizes how much these YouTubers earn on their videos.

Home Feed

The home feed is the first page a user sees when they open the app. This is where they will see a variety of content being placed on their feed by YouTube, most of which will be determined by what you watch the most, who you are subscribed to, and what's trending. YouTube will recommend videos that the algorithm thinks you will enjoy watching based on the previously mentioned factors and more. That way, you do not need to search much on the app to find something you would be interested in viewing.

Video Content

YouTube is the biggest source of video content available, with 500 hours of video being uploaded every minute and 720,000 hours being uploaded daily. It is almost impossible to run out of things to watch on YouTube and this can make it very addictive. From dancing videos to tutorials and just general entertainment, you can find anything that would interest you on this platform (and lots of it).

There is a significant amount of content designed for children between the age of 4 – 10 years old. If your child spends a lot of time on YouTube, it would be helpful to see whether or not they are being advertised to. Children are very impressionable, and YouTube has had to put a lot of effort into restricting ads to children below the age of 18.

Subscribing

Subscribing is a feature of YouTube that allows you to essentially "follow" various content creators you enjoy. Once you subscribe to a YouTube channel, it becomes quite common for their content to be recommended to you as you scroll through the homepage. This will also encourage YouTube to recommend videos like those that you follow, to encourage you to stay on the app with more content that appeals to you.

Upon subscribing, users can set up a feature that "notifies" them once their favorite YouTubers have uploaded. This sends a pop-up directly to your phone, tablet, or computer that informs you a YouTuber you've subscribed to has uploaded a new video. This can often draw a user back to the app even if they were not using it prior, and it is a clever way of keeping viewers invested.

Shorts

YouTube has adopted a feature that is essentially the same as TikTok and Instagram's "Reels". This feature allows anyone to upload short-format videos that a user can scroll through and be shown the most popular content available at any given time. This is not entirely based on anything other than interests and what is trending at any given time.

The adoption of this format is to keep as many people using YouTube as possible, and since YouTube is already a video-based platform, it is a feature that a lot of its users already engage with using TikTok. It is not as popular as TikTok though, and it is generally used as a way for YouTubers to keep in touch with their subscribers when they aren't posting longer videos to their YouTube channels.

Live Streams

Live streaming is becoming more and more popular, especially within the niche of gaming. Content creators who specialize in gaming find a lot of value out of streaming because their audiences can engage with them in real-time about the game that they are playing. Allowing viewers to compete for the streamer's attention, hoping to be mentioned.

Additionally, viewers can donate money alongside a message that the streamer is usually guaranteed to see and respond to. These donations can range from $1 to $10,000 and although it is uncommon for streamers to receive such large donations, there are the occasional wealthy viewers that choose to do so. The most common donation amounts are from $1 to $100.

As your child may be engaging with this format of content, it may be good to regulate their viewing. It is quite common for streams to run 8 or more hours per day on certain occasions, including streams of up to 24 hours or more depending on the event and reason for the stream (such as charity events by streamers). It may be important to track the donations your child is making in the event they are watching live streams by disconnecting any credit cards associated with their YouTube account or by limiting their spending.

Creator Studio

YouTubers who upload to the platform use the Creator Studio. The Creator Studio allows them to see all the videos they have uploaded alongside the view count and the number of likes their video has received. YouTubers also get access to a variety of other demographics such as the age range of their viewers, the locations of their viewers, which device their viewers are watching on, and a large amount of other data to help them in their quest for content creation.

Fortunately, YouTube does not give out this information on a personal level, and YouTubers cannot get access to any specific users' data. It is all generalized once certain numbers are accumulated.

Controversies

Today, most controversies around YouTube happen between the company and its community of content creators, as there are many decisions made by YouTube regularly that their creator community may or may not agree with.

Something that is a threat to the platform now is bots, as it is quite common for bots to masquerade as popular YouTubers in comment sections and encourage people to enter various competitions for free money when in reality these accounts steal personal information once the links have been clicked. It is unsafe to click and follow links that aren't from the official video's description as they can easily be linked to various scams. I would encourage you to notify your children of this danger and I would encourage you to use YouTube and see what dangers you may observe for yourself.

8. Twitter

Twitter is one of the most politically and socially influential apps in the world. Basically, it is a more sociable form of Reddit, in which most of the app is based on text-based posts and a few images or videos. It is a platform on which users can directly upload their thoughts and opinions and receive engagement as likes and comments.

Twitter was founded in 2006 with the purpose "to connect its users and allow them to share their thoughts with their followers and others through the use of hashtags". It is a discussion-based platform and is often categorized as "micro-blogging" as people share their thoughts thro "Tweets" (which is the term for a post on Twitter). It currently has around 400 million users worldwide, with nearly 400,000 tweets made per minute.

Twitter is very well known amongst the internet community as it has a massive impact on various sectors of our society. An example of this would be the ban of President Donald Trump from the platform. Regardless of your stance on this topic, it is safe to say that Twitter has a massive impact on the information that its users are exposed to.

Twitter is well known for banning users for their opinions, ideas, beliefs, and anything that may not align with the company's political and social agenda. The users of Twitter engage this mentality themselves by policing users, and this can often result in large-scale bullying or attacks on different people and ideas. This is commonly known as "canceling."

Mostly, Twitter is straightforward with how users share their thoughts via tweets and other users interact with those tweets. How most Twitter users engage with these features will give you an idea of how people interact with one another as well as the potential value and dangers that may come from it.

Tweeting

The key feature of Twitter is the ability to tweet mini blogs of 280 characters or less. This means that there is a restriction to how much you can include in a single tweet, and if you want a tweet to include more characters than this, you will have to create a 'thread' in which a user simply responds to their tweet with another tweet, adding to the length of the former and allowing a user to explore more detailed ideas. A user can add as much as they would like to their initial tweet, but it will not show until the initial tweet has been opened by a reader. Often, people may not know there is more to the tweet if they don't open the thread, thus resulting in reactions and responses to the initial tweet.

This does not make Twitter an excellent platform for constructive conversations amongst users because there is quite a severe word limit and flow to extended conversations. It is quite common for users to react to an initial tweet without considering the thread and as a platform that focuses heavily on short and often controversial tweets; it is part of the culture not to tweet anything too long.

I would advise keeping an eye on what your child tweets and the tweets that appear on their homepage. A lot of the content on Twitter is designed to get engagement by being divisive or controversial and this is bait to keep users engaging with the app. Your child may also be tweeting divisive thoughts to gain a following, and this can put their account at risk of bullying.

Trending

Twitter has a feature that allows users to see what is trending both in their country and around the world. Certain hashtags can pop up depending on the circumstances around various scenarios. It is common for users to see what is trending and begin engaging with other tweets and users before fully understanding the depth of the trend.

Trends are a quick way for users to potentially gain a larger following and post a tweet that gets a lot of engagement. Identifying what's trending allows you to see where many Twitter users are spending their time.

Additionally, Twitter also covers what is most popular in various aspects of global news, often linking to trending sources in entertainment news, political news, corporate news, or anything else that may be trending. Various topics can ripple into trends that users then turn into a hashtag and start engaging with.

Because trends are always changing, taking an interest in topics that your child takes interest in could help navigate their opinions on various topics. It is not easily possible to limit a user's exposure to trends on Twitter but the best thing that can be done is a constructive conversation to avoid the opinions of other users heavily affecting your child.

Replies

Besides liking tweets, users can reply to the tweets that others make. This is a huge source of engagement on the platform and many users try to get as many replies to a tweet as possible (this will boost the likelihood of more people seeing the tweet). Predictably, users try to either tweet thoughts that are very agreeable to the general population of Twitter, or tweets that are very controversial to the population of Twitter as a means of stirring up emotions of people who may come across the tweet.

It can be very desirable to aim for large amounts of engagement on Twitter as it provides many users with temporary virality and shows that it is attainable for any user, regardless of their follower counts.

Retweet

Retweeting is a feature that allows users to repost or re-share any tweet that they come across. Whether it is because it is relatable, controversial, or funny. Retweeting content that a user enjoys to their following is a great way to get an engagement on an original tweet. Additionally, users can retweet and attach a comment of their own to the tweet, expanding upon the initial tweet and often making it more engaging. It is quite common for a retweet with a comment to go viral instead of the original tweet itself.

This is a very effective way to share ideas and opinions that were not expressed by you, but it can easily result in seeing a tweet that you may not have wanted to see because a user you follow chose to retweet it. It is also common for tweets to appear on your feed based on the people you follow and the tweets that they like or retweet. By following a user, you can be exposed to the content that they see as Twitter will believe you are interested in the same content. This can lead to harmful content unwillingly appearing on a user's page.

Knowing who your child is following on Twitter and the content they engage with would be important in understanding how the app is influencing their opinions, beliefs, and social position. If you create an account and follow your child, you will frequently see the content that they are engaging with and the tweets they may be posting themselves.

Direct Messaging

Direct messaging on Twitter can be used to message friends (users who follow one another) as well as anyone else on the platform if they have the option for anyone to message them activated. Fortunately, direct messaging from any account can be de-activated so that only mutual followers can communicate directly.

Direct messages are used to continue a conversation that takes place in the replies section of a tweet as it is quite common for users to want to directly and secretly bully users with harmful words. Additionally, people use direct messages to send spam to other users like on Instagram. If users click on the links, they often acquire their Twitter information and begin spamming more people on the newly hacked account. Notifying your children of this threat can make them weary of clicking on random links through any of their direct messages.

Spaces

Twitter Space is a new feature on the app that allows users to commune in groups on conversational topics and speak to one another using a group voice chat. Hosts of the conversation have control of who is allowed to speak and when to avoid harmful behavior taking place directly between users.

Culture

One of the most prominent cultural phenomena that have come out of Twitter is the rise of "cancel culture". I will not be addressing whether or not cancel culture is a good or bad thing as it possesses qualities that are both beneficial to the exposure of harmful behavior but can quickly turn into a witch hunt for people who do not conform to the social standards of Twitter users.

The danger of canceled culture can come through consistent participation in the trend. It can become very easy and enjoyable to join in on the "canceling" of an individual without a full understanding of the scenario or even whether it's true. Often, claims can be made on Twitter and a social response can arise before the mentioned canceled individual is even aware or able to clarify the situation.

Many users on Twitter enjoy canceling others based on their opinions, beliefs, or tweets from the past. This can often be harmful for no reason other than an attempt to force social compliance and express anger.

Participating in cancel culture can be very harmful but also powerful (in scenarios such as exposing people like Harvey Weinstein). The likelihood of coming across these trends is very high on Twitter and even if our child is participating, simply seeing the behavior can affect how your child thinks. Staying up to date with the large-scale trends that take place on the app can help when trying to address how it may affect your child. Conversations can be had to ensure they aren't solely being influenced by opinions they come across on social media.

Something that is lesser known is the prevalence of bots on the app. Bots are not as simplistic as you may believe them to be. Different nations use bots to influence users' thinking and engage with trends. This is usually done in harmful ways in which a reply to a tweet may be controversial solely for upsetting those who come across it and enticing them to engage with an argument. However, they are unaware that a bot with the sole purpose of engaging certain topics stated this, and it is unknown how many conflicts take place on the app because of this alone.

This connects to a recent controversy that took place with Elon Musk attempting to purchase the company. He publicized that the reason he may want to step away from the deal is because of the lack of information around how many users on the platform are bots, as this could decimate the value of the company depending on the reported numbers.

Bots are used to push political perspectives on the app, as in the United States; there is a clear discrepancy between people who identify as Republicans or Democrats. The stirring controversy between these two groups on Twitter can have a large impact on real-world behavior and the spread of certain dis/information can cause a true impact on political results. Using bots to start these arguments is a guaranteed way of influencing thinking by bringing up certain topics in the first place.

This leads to the next step of influence that the app holds in its capacity to ban various users, depending on what they tweet and what their opinions are. If these opinions do not fall into the social acceptance of certain political affiliations, information can be withheld from users and claimed to be "misinformation". But Twitter is not one hundred percent capable of determining what is and is not the misinformation. Thus, they use the private interest of certain topics to determine which information they allow. Information that goes against the interest of its investors may cause it being flagged or removed from the platform.

Porn is also quite prominent on Twitter and easy to come across. Age restrictions can be set to ensure it does not appear on accounts that are too young, but the app can often miss nude content and not flag it. It might appear through retweets or as suggested content.

I would highly advise using Twitter yourself and following your child on the platform if they use it. It is very influential to thinking and is often very charged with the discussion of socio-economic issues and political issues that most of the users discussing these topics are not qualified to discuss.

10. Conclusion

Social media was generally developed to deepen human connection and communication, but these good intentions dwindle once profits become the primary focus of these corporations. With each platform that is created, different psychological effects appear depending on the applications, and as time goes on, we continue to have more controversial discussions. This means that social media has both positive and negative effects on people and understanding these social media can help you and your children functionally navigate these effects.

New social media is always being developed and there are many ways of communicating beyond the applications that I have discussed in this book. People on average spend about two and a half hours on social media each day (some people spend over 4+ hours) and this number is most likely going to increase with immersion. Our youth is the target market for these developments and this may enhance social media's effect on mental health.

Keeping in touch with trends and news to see what users on the platforms may be engaging with can help you identify threats that may appear on the platforms. Being aware of large-scale decisions that the companies make can give you an idea of what their intentions are and how they will adapt their apps to match these intentions (one of the largest intentions being to increase revenue).

Bullying is very prevalent on these platforms and may easily go unnoticed if you are not aware of your child's activity on social media. The culture of apps also puts certain types of content in the spotlight and some of this may negatively affect how youth think and interact with others. Content is very rapid and attention spans are decreasing as rewards are provided for scrolling through short and often semi-entertaining content.

Using social media yourself is one of the most effective ways of gauging how it affects its users and it will keep you up to date with trends and controversies being discussed. This makes it important to speak with your kids honestly about the social media streams they spend time on and the discussed effects that the platforms may have. Conversations are going to become more and more controversial and it will be essential to understand the context of certain developments to ensure a well-informed point of view.

Speaking to other parents will also be a valuable way to manage the impact of the platforms. Building your community around how you communicate these issues to your children may provide ideas for how they can be addressed in a non-invasive manner and may make you more confident in understanding the topic before speaking to your child.

References

- Braden Becker (2017). *27 Instagram Hacks, Tips, & Features Everyone Should Know About.* [online] Hubspot.com. Available at: https://blog.hubspot.com/marketing/instagram-features-tricks.

- Carr, J. (2020). *TikTok is a magnet for paedos - it's a scandal our kids are still allowed on.* [online] The Sun. Available at: https://www.thesun.co.uk/tech/10916333/tiktok-magnet-paedophiles-scandal/.

- DSouza, D. (2022). *What Is TikTok?* [online] Investopedia. Available at: https://www.investopedia.com/what-is-tiktok-4588933#:~:text=TikTok%20is%20a%20popular%20social.

- Elsesser, K. (2021). *Here's How Instagram Harms Young Women According To Research.* [online] Forbes. Available at: https://www.forbes.com/sites/kimelsesser/2021/10/05/heres-how-instagram-harms-young-women-according-to-research/?sh=f056350255ae [Accessed 25 Sep. 2022].

- Facebook for Business. (n.d.). *Facebook Stories: An Introduction for Content Creators.* [online] Available at: https://www.facebook.com/business/learn/lessons/facebook-stories-creators.

- GCFGlobal.org. (n.d.). *The Now: What is Reddit?* [online] Available at: https://edu.gcfglobal.org/en/thenow/what-is-reddit/1/.

- Google (n.d.). *Our Approach – How Google Search Works.* [online] Google Search - Discover How Google Search Works. Available at: https://www.google.com/search/howsearchworks/our-approach/#:~:text=Google%27s%20mission%20is%20to%20org anize.

- Hambrick | @MyiaChristine, M. (2017). *Opinion: Snapchat culture distorts reality, adds no real value to social life.* [online] The Reveille. Available at: https://www.lsureveille.com/daily/opinion-snapchat-culture-distorts-reality-adds-no-real-value-to-social-life/article_8cad0178-0824-11e7-800c-dfd6b52ee73f.html.

- Instagram (2022). *What is Instagram? | Instagram Help Center.* [online] Instagram.com. Available at: https://help.instagram.com/424737657584573.

- Ltd, B.I.P. (n.d.). *Skill Finder.* [online] www.skillfinder.com.au. Available at: https://www.skillfinder.com.au/course/what-is-the-main-purpose-of-twitter#:~:text=Twitter%20is%20a%20social%20media [Accessed 25 Sep. 2022].

- Mcfarlane, G. (2020). *How Facebook, Twitter, Social Media Make Money From You.* [online] Investopedia. Available at: https://www.investopedia.com/stock-analysis/032114/how-facebook-twitter-social-media-make-money-you-twtr-lnkd-fb-goog.aspx.

- New (2016). *10 New YouTube Features Added to Improve User Experience - Small Business Trends.* [online] Small Business Trends. Available at: https://smallbiztrends.com/2015/07/new-youtube-features-2015.html.

- Orge Castellano (2019). *Instagram: Beware of The Toxic Culture Behind It - Orge Castellano - Medium.* [online] Medium. Available at: https://orge.medium.com/instagram-beware-of-the-toxic-culture-behind-it-7ecff96108b4.

- Peard, L. (2018). *A List of the Latest Facebook Features You Might Not Know Exist!* [online] Social Media & Influencer Marketing Speaker, Consultant & Author. Available at: https://nealschaffer.com/facebook-features/#8-3-messages [Accessed 25 Sep. 2022].

- Pocket-lint (2022). *What is Snapchat Plus, how much is it and what's it include?* [online] www.pocket-lint.com. Available at: https://www.pocket-lint.com/apps/news/snapchat/162265-snapchat-plus-price-features-what-does-it-include-how-does-it-work-subscription [Accessed 25 Sep. 2022].

- Rodriguez, S. (2019). *Inside Facebook's 'cult-like' workplace, where dissent is discouraged and employees pretend to be happy all the time.* [online] CNBC. Available at: https://www.cnbc.com/2019/01/08/facebook-culture-cult-performance-review-process-blamed.html.

- Shepherd, J. (2022). *30 Essential Facebook Statistics You Need To Know In 2022.* [online] The Social Shepherd. Available at: https://thesocialshepherd.com/blog/facebook-

statistics#:~:text=The%20largest%20Facebook%20audience%20
in.

- Silberling, A. (2021). *Following lawsuits, Snapchat pulls its controversial speed filter*. [online] TechCrunch. Available at: https://techcrunch.com/2021/06/17/following-lawsuits-snapchat-takes-down-controversial-speed-filter/ [Accessed 25 Sep. 2022].

- Snapchat (n.d.). *Snapchat Support*. [online] support.snapchat.com. Available at: https://support.snapchat.com/en-GB/article/integrated-features [Accessed 25 Sep. 2022].

- Webwise.ie. (2014). *Explained: What is Facebook? -*. [online] Available at: https://www.webwise.ie/parents/explained-what-is-facebook-2/#:~:text=Facebook%20is%20a%20website%20which.

- Webwise.ie. (2015). *Explained: What is YouTube?* [online] Available at: https://www.webwise.ie/parents/what-is-youtube/#:~:text=YouTube%20is%20a%20video%20sharing.

- Webwise.ie. (2018). *Explainer: What is Snapchat? -*. [online] Available at: https://www.webwise.ie/parents/explainer-what-is-snapchat-2/#:~:text=Snapchat%20is%20a%20mobile%20messaging.

- www.pallasweb.com. (n.d.). *Lessons for social media websites from Instagram controversy - Pallasart Web Design News | Austin TX*. [online] Available at: https://www.pallasweb.com/blog/lessons-for-social-media-websites-from-instagram-controversy.html [Accessed 25 Sep. 2022].

- www.youtube.com. (2021). *The Tragic Tale of Reddit*. [online] Available at: https://www.youtube.com/watch?v=0SQ-TJKPPIg&t=1023s [Accessed 25 Sep. 2022].

Printed in Great Britain
by Amazon

22011668R00029